A FIELD SUNFLOWERS

by Neil Johnson

Cartwheel
·B·O·O·K·S·®

SCHOLASTIC INC.
New York Toronto London Auckland Sydney

I am most grateful to my friend,
Gordon Boogaerts,
for his constant generosity
during the production of this book!

ISBN 0-590-96549-2

Copyright © 1997 by Neil Johnson.
CARTWHEEL BOOKS and the CARTWHEEL BOOKS logo are registered trademarks
of Scholastic Inc.
All rights reserved. Published by Scholastic Inc.

12 11 10 9 8 7   8 9/9 0 1 2/0

Printed in the U.S.A.   60

First Scholastic printing, April 1997

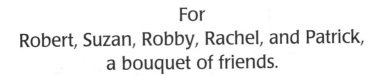

For
Robert, Suzan, Robby, Rachel, and Patrick,
a bouquet of friends.

Gordon looks out over his field and decides this year he will plant something different. First, he must prepare the ground for planting. The **disc plow** loosens the hard-packed soil to let it breathe.

The **planter** plants one seed at a time in long rows that stretch from one side of the field to the other. It growls as it moves back and forth, back and forth all afternoon.

After only one day, the soil's warmth and moisture have helped each seed to **germinate**, or sprout. A tiny plant called a **cotyledon** pushes its way out of the seed and up through the soil. Rain helps to speed up the process. About ten days after germination, the cotyledons reach their destination — daylight!

From the sunflower cotyledons, the first leaves appear. The once tender little plants are now growing taller, bigger, and stronger with each passing day. Although six weeks have passed since germination, the plants have a long way to grow to reach their adult height.

As they grow, the sunflower plants seek the sun. Each morning, the tip of every plant in the field points toward the exact spot where the sun rises. As the sun moves overhead, the plants turn with it until they bid the sun good-bye at dusk. Overnight, the plants turn back to the east and prepare to greet the morning sun again. This movement is called **phototropism**.

The plants grow between 6 and 8 feet tall. Heavy **buds** begin to form. At this time, the **stalk fibers** stiffen, making the plant stronger. From now on, the plants will face the sunrise. Finally, one dawn, the sun casts its rosy light on the field's first bloom.

Within a week, a field of sunflowers shines in the sun.
Each sunflower plant has only one bloom or **head**.

Word of Gordon's field spreads quickly. Soon people drive out from the city to see for themselves. Families bring their children for picnics. Photographers shoot roll after roll of film. Artists work to capture the beauty in oil, pastel, and watercolor.

One day, a path is cut. The narrow walkway winds its way through the blooms and allows sunflower lovers to feel almost as though they are a part of the field.

Each head of a sunflower is, in fact, a cluster of hundreds of small flowers called **florets**. A sunflower seed cannot be formed without **pollination**. Pollination occurs when a grain of **pollen** is moved from the floret's **anther** to the **stigma**. Sunflowers depend on bees and many other insects to carry the pollen to the stigma.

Gordon is very proud. To celebrate the glory of
the sunflowers, he hosts a dinner party underneath
the oak trees in his backyard next to the field.

The blooms last for about two weeks before they fade.

Each bloom is now full of hundreds of seeds, each containing the potential to be another tall sunflower plant. But, Gordon decides not to harvest the heads for their seeds. Though the plants will die, the seeds in the flowers' heads are still very much alive. The once beautiful field becomes a gigantic bird feeder for cardinals, red-winged blackbirds, mockingbirds, doves, and other birds.

The end?